GRANTWRITING STEP BY STEP

*A Simple, straightforward guidebook
for getting the money you need.*

By

Anne H. Holt, Ph.D.

GRANTWRITING STEP BY STEP

Introduction

Successful grant-writing involves careful advance planning and preparation. It takes time to coordinate this planning and research, organize and write your proposal. It takes time to collect letters of support and other information requested by a funder and submit your proposal exactly as requested by your funder.

Planning and research is vital to the grant-writing process. Your well-thought-out preliminary work will simplify the writing stage. A well-written and complete proposal follows the basic steps outlined in this booklet.

Once you write one complete proposal, you can modify it as needed to approach other funders for help on the same project. Also, some of your work will cross-over and help you to you write grants for other projects.

Make sure the targeted grant maker's goals and objectives match your grantseeking purposes. Study the grantor's guidelines until you clearly understand the grant maker's funding targets before you write your proposal. Make sure your organization works in the geographical area of the funder's interest. Use the grant maker's words in your proposal whenever possible.

Always follow the **exact specifications** of the grant makers in their applications and guidelines. It is hard to stress this point enough.

It helps to know that the first "weeding out" of grant applications includes someone checking to make sure the applicant followed instructions **exactly**.

Grant makers, often referred to as "grantors" receive a large number of applications, so even the most trivial point of their requirements you might decide to ignore, could eliminate your proposal.

In seminars I often stress this point by saying "if the grantor specifies pink paper for your proposal and you find your office supply store has paper in two shades of pink, you must call the grantor and find out which of the two shades you should use."

This sounds as if I am stretching a point, and I am, but only a little. Always remember – if a grantor has many proposals – he or she will certainly be looking for a way to reduce them to a manageable number.

Organize your proposal exactly as instructed in the guidelines, pay attention to detail and specifications, use concise, persuasive wording, and request reasonable but adequate funding.

Think your budget request through carefully. Your grant will be eliminated just as quickly for asking for inadequate funds to do the job as it will be eliminated for submitting an obviously padded budget.

Follow the instructions in this workbook and you will build an information and skill base to find the money your organization needs to fund its projects.

Use these basic steps to guide you:

1. Prove, through careful, checkable research, that you have a significant need or problem.

2. Deliver a solution to the problem you have outlined, based on your experience, ability, logic, and imagination.

3. Reflect careful planning, extensive research and vision.

4. Carefully study all targeted grant makers. Read their funding purposes and priorities and applicant eligibility to determine that their goals and objectives match yours.

5. **Request a copy of a successful grant if possible.**

6. Do not limit your funding request to one source.

7. In many cases you can contact the grant maker, **before** you write your proposal to be sure you clearly understand their guidelines.

8. Present your proposal in the appropriate and complete format, and include all required attachments.

9. State clearly and concisely your organization's needs, goals and objectives.

10. Have someone edit your writing for accuracy, spelling and grammar.

11. Have someone audit your grant budget.

12. If needed, hire a consultant (to be paid in the grant) with the required credentials, especially if you need a professional evaluator.

13. Always follow the exact specifications of the grant makers in their applications, requests for proposals (RFPs) and guidelines.

14. Always thoroughly cover, with financial reports and resumes, your organization's accountability and the competence of your staff, volunteers and board members.

15. If you are not awarded the grant you apply for, contact the funder and request feedback about your proposal's strengths and weaknesses.

Build a Project Notebook for Grant Writing

In a large three-ring-binder,
place dividers titled as follows:

1. **Mission Statement and organization description:** including job descriptions and current resumes of key personnel.

2. **FINANCES & LEGALITIES: (a)** An up-to-date asset and liabilities statement, a budget for current year and any years involved in proposed grants. (b) Income and expense statement for current and past year. (c)Current copies of Employer ID number and Duns number, (d)501 C (3) letter, (e) copies of 990 filing and state charity registration and/or corporate filing if applicable.

3. If you plan to apply for state or federal grants, you will need to register with **SAMS.**

4. **Management:** Your board of directors names and contact information, short bios and affiliations for each, include up-to-date committee lists with contact and short description of duties.

5. **Activities:** Description of your organization's activities and on-going projects, include detailed descriptions and examples of your marketing plans and materials such as brochures, posters, logos, giveaways and public service announcements.

6. **New Project:** Project Description including materials and resources. Who will benefit and why your community needs this service. Include research proving this need.

7. **New Project Approach:** This will cover materials stating this projects goals, objectives and activities proposed.

8. **New Project Management/Implementation Plan:** Suggest strategies for leading and managing the activities of this project, how funds and staff will be allocated.

9. **Evaluation Methodology:** Plans and tools for measuring results, showing this project's impact on the community problem or need.

10. **Publicity:** Plans for publicity campaign before and during program to gain community and funders support.

You will not need all of the listed information for completing every grant you complete, but having it at your fingertips will save time with every grant you write.

Preliminary Proposal or Grant Query Letter

Many grant makers accept grant applications by invitation only, and require potential grant recipients to submit preliminary proposals in the form of inquiry letters in order to be invited to submit a full proposal.

Inquiry or "query" letters are designed to convince the grant maker to consider your request. They provide you an opportunity to give the grant maker a snapshot of your proposed project/program.

Read guidelines carefully, then read them again. Be sure to establish **in writing** a connection between your proposal's goals and the grant maker's priorities.

Focus on detail, clarity, and conciseness, while conveying the full impact your project will make on the need or problem you address.

Be sure to mention how you will evaluate your project and how you will give the grant maker credit.

Find the name of a person to address your inquiry letter to even if you must call the funder's office and ask. Type your letter on your organization's stationary.

CAREFULLY FOLLOW ANY SPECIFIC INSTRUCTIONS GIVEN BY A FUNDER

**In some form, funders want the following information.
Keep it as concise as possible
Use no more than two pages or as required
in an application form furnished by the funder.**

1. The mission of your organization.

2. The purpose of your request

3. How your request fits the grant maker's funding priorities

4. Your organization's total annual operating budget

5. Your organization's fiscal year dates.

6. Total proposed project/program budget

7. Grant amount being requested for your project

8. Matching funds committed from other funding sources or on hand.

9. Proposed grant project/program time frame (beginning and ending dates)

10. Proof of your organization's tax exempt status

11. A concise narrative or a synopsis of the proposed project/program, that covers the purpose of the request, the problem or need being addressed, and how you will approach solving the identified problem or need.

12. State the population or community served by your organization and how your project or program will effect long-term change.

Full Proposal

There are different forms and formats for full funding proposals. Every funder or grant maker has different guidelines and priorities, deadlines and timetables.

Always follow the exact specifications of the grant makers in their applications, Requests for Proposals (RFPs) and guidelines.

Full proposals include a cover letter, cover sheet, narrative, budget, organizational and staff qualifications, conclusion and appendices, as follows:

Cover Sheet – short - a case statement and executive summary

Needs Assessment - a concise demonstration of the specific situation, opportunity, problem, issue, need, and the community your proposal addresses.

Your program goals and objectives - a succinct description of the proposed project/program's outcome and accomplishments in measurable terms, and how it matches the funder's interests.

Your methodology - a rational, direct, chronological description of the proposed project and the process used to achieve your proposed outcomes and accomplishments.

Evaluation - your plan for meeting performance goals and completing the program/project. Who will design collection instruments and collect data? Will you need a consultant?

Budget/Funding Requirements - a realistic budget with a detailed explanation of the funding request, committed matching funds, evidence of sound fiscal management, and a long-term funding plan.

Qualifications - your organization's background, its funding history, board involvement and its capacity to carry out your proposal. Program staff and their qualifications.

Media Exposure – How do you plan to use the media—newspaper, TV, Radio, brochures or Internet to get the word out about your project and attract more partners and participants. How will you let the public know who is funding your project?

Conclusion - a brief summary of your proposal.

Appendices - additional attachments required by the funder, such as proof of tax exempt status, organizational and financial documents, staff/board lists, staff resumes, support or commitment letters.

Finally - present your full proposal neatly, professionally, and in an organized package.

Type all proposals. Write, organize and present your proposal in the order listed in the application and guidelines.

Carefully include any required attachments, but <u>only</u> include the information and materials specifically requested by the grant maker.

Unless required, do not include an index or table of contents, or bind the proposal.

Be sure to sign your proposal in blue ink and submit the number of copies requested by the grant maker ---

EXACTLY AS REQUESTED.

BUDGETING

Again, follow the funder's guidelines EXACTLY.

If you use a different format for financial reporting, convert your figures to the grantor's format.

If you have questions about your funder's definition of "in kind" and/or "matching funds" telephone his or her office and ask for clarification.

Do not "pad" your budget in case of unforeseen expenses. Seek bids for equipment, supplies, etc. Ask your vendors to fax or e-mail or mail bids to you and retain them in case your funder questions a figure.

Be careful to request funding for everything you will need to accomplish your goals.

If you already own the van or machine you need to accomplish your goals, make sure your funder knows that and will not possibly think you accidentally left the expense out.

It is as bad to ask for too little money to accomplish your goals as it is to ask for an unreasonably large amount.

Note that most funders either state no administration costs will be paid or specify a figure you may include in your budget.

If your funder does not specify a figure for administration expense, unless you are a government agency with an agreed upon figure, ten (10) percent is a generally accepted figure.

Do not allow yourself to get discouraged if you do not get every grant you write. No one can. You can only win grants if you continue to write them. If you have faith in your ideas and continue to develop them – keep finding and applying for related grants -- you will get the money you need.

═══════════════════════════════════════

NOTE: SEE THE APPENDIX FOR A MODEL NARRATIVE BUDGET

Project Development Questionnaire
For Grant Writing

Describe a need or bad condition that exists today and you would like to change (create an image).

What exact problems does this need or difficulty cause?

Why does this happen?

To whom is it happening? (Give statistics from federal census figures if possible). If you gather the statistics yourself, explain fully how you collected them.)

Why do you think this problem exists?

What idea do you have for a project that will correct the unwanted problem or condition?

What is the purpose of your project?

Give 2 goals – Two changes you must accomplish to make your project successful.

Goal 1 –

Goal 2 –

Give two objectives (activities) that must be accomplished to reach each of your goals.

a. Goal 1: Objective 1

b. Goal 1: Objective 2

c. Goal 2: Objective 1

d. Goal 2: Objective 2

**How will your project re-shape the original condition or correct the
original problem?**

Who will you partner/collaborate with on your project?

How much will it cost to do the project well? (consult the model budget)

How can you make your project sustainable? Can you eliminate the problem completely or will you need to continue your project into the future?

Will your project be replicable? Explain how your idea can help solve the same problems in other places.

RESOURSES

Grant Research Websites

Educational Grant Writing Links

AcademicInfo
AcademicInfo.net features education resources for current teachers (research tools, writing guides, journals, books, and more) in addition to study information for potential teachers.

Afterschool.gov
Afterschool.gov offers one-stop access to government resources that support after school programs. You can find information to help you understand the issues that face kids and teens or fund, start and operate an after school program.

Center for Community and Economic Development
Helps communities apply and transfer multi-disciplinary knowledge to help people understand community change and identify opportunities.

Edventures!
PCS Edventures is a provider of fun hands-on science, technology, engineering, and math (STEM) curriculum for schools, after-school, and home education!

Grant Wrangler
This web site provides online resources for K-12 schools, students, librarians, and teachers searching for funding.

SchoolGrants
SchoolGrants was created as a way to share grant information with PK-12 educators, and helps ease grant writing fears by providing tips to those who need them.

The Education Trust

The Education Trust works for the high academic achievement of all students at all levels, kindergarten through college, and forever closing the achievement gaps that separate low-income students and students of color from other youth.

US Department of Education

This site offers an abundant amount of information including grants & contracts, financial aid, and educational resources.

Government Grant Resources

Catalog of Federal Domestic Assistance

The CFDA contains information on federal grant programs that includes application procedures, eligibility, and deadlines. A search feature is included as well

Centers for Disease Control and Prevention

CDC serves as the national focus for developing and applying disease prevention and control, environmental health, and health promotion and education activities designed to improve the health of the people of the United States. The site includes funding opportunities, health related topics, and much more.

CDC National Prevention Information Network

NPIN produces, collects, catalogs, processes, stocks, and disseminates materials and information on HIV/AIDS, STD's, and tuberculosis to organizations and people working in those disease fields.

Chief Grants - Public Safety Resource

Specializing exclusively in grant training and consulting services for Public Safety Agencies in the US with special emphasis on Department of Homeland Security grant funding streams.

Division of Cost Allocation, US Department of Health & Human Services
For information about indirect costs. On this web page you will find contact info for division & personnel

Dun & Bradstreet
The D&B D-U-N-S Number is a unique nine-digit identification sequence, which provides unique identifiers of single business entities, while linking corporate family structures together. In today's global economy, the D&B D-U-N-S Number has become the standard for keeping track of the world's businesses.

Federal Register
"The *Federal Register* is the official daily publication for Rules, Proposed Rules, and Notices of Federal agencies and organizations, as well as Executive Orders and other Presidential Documents." The site includes a search feature as well.

FedWorld.gov
The FedWorld.gov web site is a gateway to government information. The site was established to serve as the online locator service for a comprehensive inventory of information disseminated by the Federal Government.

FirstGov
This is the only official U.S. Government portal to 47 million pages of government information, services, and online transactions. The site offers a powerful search engine that searches every word of every U.S. government document in a quarter of a second or less.

GrantsNet
GrantsNet is an Internet application tool created by the Department of Health and Human Services (DHHS) Office of Grants Management (OGM) for finding and exchanging information about HHS and other Federal grant programs.

National Congress for Community Economic Development

NCCED represents over 3,600 community development corporations (CDCs) across America. CDC's produce affordable housing and create jobs through business and commercial development activities.

National Institutes of Health

The National Institutes of Health is one of the world's foremost medical research centers, and the Federal focal point for medical research in the U.S. This web site includes health information, grant opportunities, news and events, and much more.

National Technology Transfer Center

On this site there are links to every US Legislative Branch, US Executive Branch, US Judicial Branch, independent government agencies, and all 50 states.

State & Local Government on the Web

If you are having trouble finding web sites that relate to your state and local government, then this is the place to go. Click on a state and related government sites are listed. There are also links to other great sites!

Nonprofit Grant Resources

Action Without Borders - Idealist.org

The Idealist is a project of the Contract Center Network, a global network of community based centers dedicated to the promotion of a better world through philanthropy, communication, and organizational action. The site provides 9,000 links to nonprofit groups throughout the world.

America's Charities

The home page for this organization describes its mission and provides links to participating charities that offer direct services for communities throughout the United States. Charities are categorized as follows: Human Services, Human Rights, Education, and Health.

CD Publications
Source for news and inside reporting from Congress, federal agencies and communities around the country.

Charity Village
This site offers more than 450 pages of information on the nonprofit world of Canada. Those who want to find work in the Canadian nonprofit sector can check the Career Center for job listings.

Children Now
Dedicated to raising consciousness related to children and children's issues, this site offers ideas and suggestions on how to get involved in helping America's children.

Chronicle of Philanthropy
This is the web site of *The Chronicle of Philanthropy*. It provides information on many areas of the philanthropy world. News articles, information on gifts and grants, fundraising, nonprofit management and technology, as well as links to other web sites are available.

Community Foundation Locator
Sponsored and maintained by the Council on Foundations, this web site is a great tool for locating a community foundation in your state. Simply click on your state for a listing!

Council on Foundations
The Council on Foundations, a nonprofit membership association of grant making foundations and corporations, provides access to more than 130 publications at this site.

Dreambuddy
Government grants and small business resources.

Empower Web
Empower Web is a great starting point that leads to numerous pages about non-profit organizations, research, funding, grants, volunteer work, and related publications.

Foundation Center
A source of information on private philanthropy in the US. The Foundation Center helps the general public understand the field of philanthropy.

Foundations Online
At Foundations Online, charity representatives can scan the list of grant giving foundations, discover how to apply for a grant, and determine what the specific foundations fund. In addition, find information about applying for government grants.

Free Management Library
The library is a free community resource to be shared and contributed to by users and readers across the world. The overall goal of the library is to provide leaders and managers basic and practical information about business, management and organizations.

Fundsnet
While this site does have pop up ads from time to time, it offers numerous links to grant funding sources from a variety of areas. There is also a message board, other related links, and daily funding announcements.

GrantSmart
GrantSmart is a resource center for and about the nonprofit community. It includes a grant maker search, a donation feature, and members of nonprofit organizations can register to become SmartMembers.

GuideStar

Guidestar provides a free searchable database of reports on the programs and finances of over 600,000 U.S. charities. Articles and news on the nonprofit arena are also available.

Grant Wrangler

A free online resource listing grants and awards for K-12 teachers, schools, and students in subject areas ranging from math and science to social studies and art. The site lists more than $81 million in grants, awards, and free resources for classrooms, youth-led initiatives, teacher professional development, and recognition.

Interactive Knowledge for Nonprofits Worldwide

Interactive Knowledge for Nonprofits Worldwide (Iknow) is a collection of online resource links to information regarding business services, education, fringe benefits, fundraising, governance, human resources, an Internet resource directory for nonprofit organizations, legal issues, legislation, strategic planning, and volunteerism.

Internet Nonprofit Center

Labeled the page with "information on more nonprofits than any other site in the world," the Internet Nonprofit Center lets users find almost any charity in the U.S. Numerous additional nonprofit web pages are offered at this award winning site.

Milano Nonprofit Management Hub

The Milano Nonprofit Management Knowledge Hub provides high-quality, current information that nonprofit managers, leaders, students, researchers, teachers, and anyone else interested in the subject can find quickly and easily.

Nonprofit Genie

Managed by C-MAP, the California Management Assistance Partnership, this site features links to online news and information, a fact finding search engine, related nonprofit books, and a bundle of links to other interesting sites.

Nonprofit Online News

Nonprofit Online News is exactly that - a source of news, information, and opinion for the online nonprofit community. Recent and past articles can be viewed, or one can subscribe to receive the article via e-mail.

Philanthropy Journal

The Philanthropy Journal is an online publication that supports the nonprofit sector. Through a daily web site and free, weekly e-newsletters, the journal delivers news that helps people better understand, support, and work in the nonprofit sector. In addition to news, we feature job openings, events calendars, and announcements about grants/gifts and people working in the sector.

Resource Links

Bureau of Justice Statistics

The goal of BJS is to collect, analyze, publish, and disseminate information on crime, criminal offenders, victims of crime, and the operation of justice systems at all levels of government.

Bureau of Transportation Statistics

The Bureau of Transportation Statistics (BTS) was created for data collection, analysis, and reporting and to ensure the most cost-effective use of transportation-monitoring resources.

Census Bureau

This is the official site of the U.S. Census Bureau whose mission is "to be the preeminent collector and provider of timely, relevant, and quality data about the public and the economy of the United States."

Census State Data Centers

The State Data Center (SDC) Program is one of the Census Bureau's longest and most successful partnerships. It is a cooperative program between the states and the Census Bureau to make data available locally to the public through a network of state agencies, universities, libraries, and regional and local governments.

FedStats

The gateway to statistics from over 100 U.S. Federal agencies! The site includes direct access to statistical data on topics of your choice. Statistical profiles of States, counties, Congressional Districts, Federal judicial districts, and much more are available.

FreeLunch.com

This site has a variety of statistical information that is available free of charge. You select information you want, and it's put into your basket. When you're finished searching, you download the contents of the basket. You do have to register to use this site, but everything is free of charge.

Kids Count

Created by the Annie E. Casey Foundation, Kids Count has compiled indicators of child well-being from the 2000 U.S. Census and created an interactive online database. Data can be viewed in the form of profiles, rankings, or raw data.

National Assessment of Educational Progress - The Nation's Report Card

The National Assessment of Educational Progress (NAEP) is the only nationally representative and continuing assessment of what America's students know and can do in various subject areas.

National Association of Counties

NACo is a full-service organization that provides an extensive line of services including legislative, research, and technical as well as public affairs assistance to its members. This site is full of county data!

National Center for Education Statistics

The NCES is the primary federal entity responsible for collecting and analyzing data that are related to education in the United States and other nations.

National Center for Health Statistics

NCHS is the Federal Government's principal vital and health statistics agency. NCHS data systems include data on vital events as well as information on health status, lifestyle and exposure to unhealthy influences, the onset and diagnosis of illness and disability, and the use of health care.

Statistical Resources on the Web

Created by the University of Michigan, this site includes statistical data on numerous subjects and locations worldwide.

Teoma.com

This search engine is wonderful for locating statistical information! Teoma.com uses "Subject Specific" techniques – Refine, Results and Resources – to find information for you. "Refine" organizes sites into naturally occurring communities that can be expanded or narrowed.

APPENDIX

Model Budget Narrative –

Budget Narrative--Personnel	Grant	Match	Total
Project Director The Project Director will be responsible for oversight of all grant activities and funds. Responsibilities will include approving purchases and Supervising personnel. The project administrator will work ___ % of his/her time for 24 months. Based on an annual salary of _____ Cost to the project will be:	$	$	$
Project Manager The Project Manager will report to the Project Director. Responsibilities include oversight of the Project at $ ___ per year. Cost to the project will be:	$	$	$
Clerical Support **(To be hired?)** will provide clerical support for the Project Director and the Project Manager. Responsibilities will include answering phones, preparing purchase orders, record keeping, typing letters, reports, and other general office duties. Cost to the project will be:	$	$	$.

(Other personnel) **(To be hired--describe job)** Cost to the project will be: $	$	$	$
Liaison (with partners) **(To be hired, furnished by partner?,** ** percentage of time devoted to project?)** At an annual salary of $ Cost to the project will be:	$	$	$

Cost to Grant $
Match $_____
Total $

Budget Narrative--Fringe Benefits	Grant	Match	Total
Fringe benefits are calculated on Big Bend Personnel at___% of salary. (partners?) Fringe benefits for employees hired under this grant are calculated at a rate of % of salary (other benefits?)			
Project Director % $?, for 24 months	$	$	$
Project Manager % of $?, for 24 months	$	$	$
Clerical Support % of $ for 24 months	$	$	$
Other % of $?, for 24 months	$	$	$
Liaison % of $ @ % for 24 months	$	$	$
Other % of $	$	$	$

Cost to Grant $
Match $_____
Total $

Special Project Expenses			
Creative Consultant--			
Project Evaluator--			

Cost to Grant $
Match $_____
Total $

Budget Narrative--Travel	Grant	Match	Total
Presentations Mileage estimate,	$	$0	$
Other Transportation	$	$0	$
One conference each year, two people attending Air Fare $400 x4 = $1,600 Hotel $300 x 4 = $1,200 Registration $200 x 4 = $ 800 Food and misc. $100 x 4 = $ 400 Total $4,000	$2,000	$2,000	$4,000

Cost to Grant $
Match $_____
Total $

Budget Narrative--Other	Grant	Match	Total
Telephone Lines and installation	$0	$	$
Telephone Service	$0	$	$
Long Distance Fees	$0	$	$
Internet Access	$0	$	$
Photocopy	$0	$	$.
Instruction Materials	$0	$	$
Other	$0	$	$

Cost to Grant $
Match $_____
Total $

Budget Narrative--Supplies	Grant	Match	Total
Office Supplies **Paper, envelopes, toner, misc.**	$	$	$
Teaching Supplies **Journals, pencils, pens,**	$	$.	$
Postage,	$	$	$
Other --Printing for Brochures	$	$	$

Cost to Grant $

Match $_____

Total $

Volunteers	Grant	Match	Total
Volunteers _____hours per month for 24 months @ $10.00 per hr. Cost to the project	$0	$	$

Cost to Grant $

Match $_____

Total $

Budget Narrative--Indirect Charges	Grant	Match	Total
Indirect Charges 8%? At a cost to the project of	$	$0	$

Cost to Grant $

Match $_____

Total $

BUDGET OVERVIEW

Budget	Grant	Match	Total
Personnel	$	$	$
Fringe Benefits	$	$	$
Special Expenses (Consultants, etc.)	$	$	$
Travel	$	$	$
Other	$	$	$
Supplies	$	$	$
Volunteers	$	$	$
Indirect Costs	$	$	$
Total Year One	$	$	$
Total Year Two	$	$	$
Total for Project	$	$	$

Anne H. Holt, Ph.D

Anne Haw Holt is a Virginian transplanted to the tiny town of Monticello, Florida. She attended Piedmont Va Community College and received her BA from Mary Baldwin College in Staunton, VA in 1989. She holds a MA in Historical Administration and Public History and a Ph.D. in History from Florida State University in Tallahassee, Florida. Her dissertation is on Florida's convict-lease system and prisons.

Anne is an accomplished storyteller and photographer. She writes fiction, poetry, and non-fiction on writing, history, parenting and Frontier Florida. Dr. Holt writes grants in support of Main Street Monticello's goals of revitalizing Monticello and Jefferson County Florida while protecting and preserving its history and culture. She teaches writing, grant writing, writing and leadership. Her fiction is historically based and family friendly.

Novels Available on Amazon:

Blanco Sol
Kindle - ASIN: B00AF9GKDC
Hardcover - ISBN-10: 080349730X
Paperback - ISBN-10: 1477814957

Riding Fence
Kindle - ASIN: B00A2NCKU8
Hardcover - ISBN-10: 0803498012
Paperback - ISBN-10: 1477814965

From Writer to Author
Kindle - ASIN: B00B78JA9G

Kendrick
Kindle - ASIN: B00BSMR2NC
Hardcover - ISBN-10: 0803496508
Paperback - ISBN-10: 1477814949

Blood Redemption
Kindle - ASIN: B009PJIIF6
Hardcover - ISBN-10: 080349890X
Paperback - ISBN-10: 1477814973

Silver Creek
Hardcover - ISBN-10: 0803496001

PRESENTATIONS:

Anne Haw Holt speaks on writing, leadership and women as heroes. She offers a short seminar on writing and revising entitled, "Prepare your Manuscript for Publication," with individual editing advice. Dr. Holt offers a seminar entitled "Introduction to Grant Writing." She presents talks entitled "How I became an Author," "Publishing My First Book," and "Marketing Your Book." in writers' conferences, libraries, schools and bookstores from Florida to Maine and west through Texas, Missouri, Kansas, Colorado to Arizona.

Contact:

Anne Haw Holt, Ph.D., c/o Monticello Trading Company, P. O. Box 323, Monticello, Fl 32344
http://www.AHHolt.com

www.ingramcontent.com/pod-product-compliance
Lightning Source LLC
Chambersburg PA
CBHW080609180526
45168CB00007B/2838